Why Science Matters

Protecting Threatened Species

Sally Morgan

Heinemann
LIBRARY

www.heinemann.co.uk/library
Visit our website to find out more information about Heinemann Library books.

To order:
☎ Phone 44 (0) 1865 888066
🖹 Send a fax to 44 (0) 1865 314091
🖥 Visit the Heinemann Bookshop at www.heinemann.co.uk/library to browse our catalogue and order online.

Heinemann Library is an imprint of Pearson Education Limited, a company incorporated in England and Wales having its registered office at Edinburgh Gate, Harlow, Essex, CM20 2JE – Registered company number: 00872828

Edited by Andrew Farrow, Megan Cotugno, and Harriet Milles
Designed by Steven Mead and Q2A Creative Solutions
Original illustrations © Pearson Education Limited
Illustrations by Gordon Hurden
Picture research by Ruth Blair
Production by Alison Parsons
Originated by Heinemann Library
Printed and bound in China by Leo Paper Products

ISBN: 978 0 4310 4069 1
13 12 11 10 09
10 9 8 7 6 5 4 3 2 1

British Library Cataloguing-in-Publication Data
Morgan, Sally
Protecting threatened species. - (Why science matters)
333.9'542
A full catalogue record for this book is available from the British Library

Acknowledgements
We would like to thank the following for allowing their pictures to be reproduced in this publication: ©Alamy **pp. 7** (Leslie Garland Picture Library), **14** (Ace Stock Limited), **23** (Penny Boyd), **24** (Marcus Gosling), **25** (Maspix-Wildside), **26** (Bryan & Cherry Alexander Photography), **27** (Mark Boulton), **28, 29** (Terry Whittaker), **30** (imagebroker), **38** (David Chapman), **46** (Hornbil Images); ©Audubon Institute **pp. 43, 44**, ©Corbis **pp. 4** (Alex Hofford/epa), **8** (Lynda Richardson), **15** (Momatiuk – Eastcott), **19** (Gary Braasch), **31** (Bettmann), **41** (China Daily/Reuters), **47** (John Carnemolla); ©Ecoscene **pp. 10** (Michael Gore), **13** (Satyendra Tiwari), **18** (Wayne Lawler), **21** (John Liddiard), **35** (Neeraj Mishra); ©FLPA **pp. 6** (Nigel Cattlin), **9** (Norman Duerden); ©Getty Images **p. 36** (Roger Tully); ©Naturepl.com **p. 16** (Angelo Gandolfi); ©Photolibrary **p. 42** (Ken Stepnell); ©Photoshot **p. 20**; ©Science Photo Library **p. 45** (David Parker). Background images supplied by ©istockphoto.

Cover photograph of a chimpanzee reproduced with permission of ©Getty Images (National Geographic). Background image courtesy of ©istockphoto.

We would like to thank Michael Bright for his invaluable assistance in the preparation of this book.

Every effort has been made to contact copyright holders of any material reproduced in this book. Any omissions will be rectified in subsequent printings if notice is given to the publishers.

Contents

Some words are printed in bold, **like this**. You can find out
what they mean in the glossary.

Why save them?

In 2007, biologists announced that the Yangtze river dolphin was "possibly **extinct**". A team of biologists from China and the United Kingdom carried out a survey of the Yangtze river in China and failed to find any dolphins. Sadly, the Yangtze river dolphin was not the only species to become extinct in 2007, although it was the most publicised. Experts estimate that as many as 55,000 species became extinct in 2007, equivalent to about 140 species a day.

Mass extinctions

Extinctions are not new. Many species become extinct naturally, due to changes in their environment. There have also been periods of mass extinctions when many species died out. For example, fossil evidence shows that 65.9 million years ago there was a catastrophic event that caused major environmental changes. It resulted in the extinction of more than half the world's species, including the dinosaurs. However, virtually all the extinctions that are occurring today are the result of human activities, such as **habitat** destruction, hunting, pollution, and climate change. The result is that species are becoming extinct 1,000 times faster than expected.

The Yangtze river dolphin was the first marine mammal to be declared extinct since the Caribbean monk seal and Japanese sea lion became extinct in the 1990s.

THE SCIENCE YOU LEARN: THE RED LIST

The International Union for Conservation of Nature (IUCN) is responsible for publishing a list of endangered species, known as the **Red List**. Their species specialists carry out detailed surveys of species and their habitats, and gather data. Each threatened species is placed in one of seven classes:

- least concern
- near threatened
- vulnerable
- endangered
- critically endangered
- extinct in wild
- extinct.

Sometimes, extinct animals are rediscovered. For example, the last specimen of the Attenborough's long-beaked echidna was seen in New Guinea in 1961, but in 2007 biologists found tracks and burrows of the echidna. Sometimes numbers increase, such as the grey whale whose population has risen to 20,000 from just a few thousand. However, the trend is for more species to move up into the endangered categories. There are 844 species classed as extinct, including 65 species that survive only in captivity (not living in the wild). However, only about 40,000 species of the known 1.8 million species have been assessed. It is likely that many species have become extinct before they have even been identified.

Why save endangered species?

Does it really matter that the Yangtze river dolphin has disappeared forever? This unique animal had a role to play in the **food web** of the river, and its disappearance has an effect on all the other animals. It is too late to save this species, but there are plenty of others that could benefit from **conservation**.

Some of the largest and best known species, such as the tiger and snow leopard, attract a lot of attention. Insects, which are among the most threatened species, are generally overlooked. However, it is often the smallest animals that have a critical role to play, such as pollinating a plant or recycling waste, and without them the whole natural community collapses. However, protecting the habitats of the larger animals also helps protect invertebrates (animals without a backbone).

Studying habitats

Back to basics

Threatened species cannot simply be saved by raising money to protect their habitat. Before it is possible to protect an animal or plant, biologists need to find out some basic facts, such as where they live, the food they eat, and what eats them.

Ecological studies

Among the most important pieces of ecological information are **biodiversity** and **population** size. Biodiversity is the number of different species living in an area, while population is the number of individuals of a species in an area. Once this information has been obtained, other data, such as the food sources and **predators**, can be gathered. All this information can be used to create a profile for each species, showing its **niche**, or job, within the community. Although there may be several similar species within a community, there is usually only one species within each niche.

This research technician is examining the plant diversity within a 1-metre quadrat.

THE SCIENCE YOU LEARN: QUADRATS AND TRANSECTS

It is impossible to count every individual plant in a habitat, so biologists sample small areas. Plants are usually sampled using quadrats and transects.

- A quadrat is a piece of apparatus that defines the area to be sampled, for example an area 0.5 by 0.5 metres (1.6 by 1.6 feet). The number and type of plants within the quadrat are recorded. A number of samples are taken, and the average calculated. The data can be used to find out the frequency and abundance of a species – that is, how often it occurs and how many are growing.

- Transects are samples that cross a habitat – for example, across a woodland glade where the light intensity varies from shade to full sun. The data from these samples can be used to show how the distribution of a plant varies with factors such as light levels, moisture, or acidity/alkalinity (pH).

INVESTIGATION: BIODIVERSITY ON THE SPORTS PITCH

It's surprising just how many different plants can be found growing in a small area. To measure the biodiversity of plants growing on a sports pitch, make a 0.5 x 0.5 metre (1.6 x 1.6 feet) quadrat and place it at random on the pitch. Make a note of the different species of plant growing in the quadrat. You do not necessarily have to know the name of each species (you could call them species A, species B, etc.), as long as you can recognise them again in another sample. Now place the quadrat at random elsewhere on the pitch and see if there are any new species of plant. Repeat this about ten times in different places, each time noting additional species. The total number of different plant species growing on the pitch is the biodiversity.

These two students are recording the number of species found within a simple quadrat made with a length of string.

Fieldwork in action

Ecological studies tend to involve a lot of observations in the field. These observations are often basic, such as what is happening, when and where. The observations are recorded and then analysed.

Timing the research

Before any field work can take place, basic knowledge of the species in question is required. For example, there is no point visiting woodland to study bats during the day, as bats are nocturnal (active only at night). Similarly, a project on primroses, bluebells, or some butterflies has to be carried out in spring when these species are active, rather than summer.

Margit Butcher, Assistant Director of Science and Stewardship with the US Nature Conservancy, examines a rare yellow pitcher plant in the Green Swamp Preserve, North Carolina, USA.

Equipment

The equipment is often very simple – just a notebook and pen to record observations, quadrats, tape measures, bags to collect samples, a magnifying glass, and small pots to collect insects and other small invertebrates. Nowadays, instruments called data loggers may be used to record temperature, pH, and moisture and oxygen content. These collect the data in such a way that it can be transferred straight onto a computer program for analysis.

More specialist equipment may include special microphones that pick up sound frequencies that are beyond the range of the human ear. For example, hydrophones can hear dolphins and whales underwater, and microphones can detect the ultrasonic squeaks of bats. Sometimes, an animal is fitted with a radio collar that emits a signal that can be picked up. This enables the ecologist to track (follow) the animal without getting too close and interfering with its behaviour.

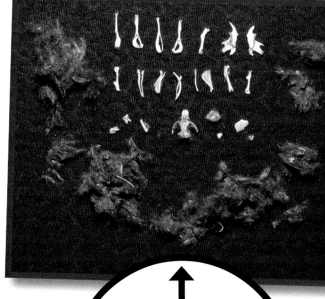

Owls are difficult to study as they are nocturnal. However, ecologists can work out which animals they have eaten by identifying the bones in the owl's faecal pellets (droppings).

CASE STUDY

Studying giraffes

For her research project, ecologist Kathy Pinkney studied giraffes living in Sweetwaters Game Reserve in Kenya. The reserve was set up to protect the threatened black rhino and ecologists wanted to find out if the rhinos were competing for food with other herbivores, such as the giraffe. Kathy spent several months watching the feeding behaviour of giraffes. Every time she saw giraffe, she recorded where they were, how many there were, and what they were eating. She also collected dung in order to find out what the giraffe had been eating. Over the study period, Kathy collected thousands of pieces of information, which were then analysed by computer.

Feeding relationships

The plants and animals living in a community depend on each other. There is a close feeding relationship between them, so the removal of one species from the community can have serious consequences for the others.

Producer and consumer

Plants are **producers** because they take light energy and use it to make their own food, such as carbohydrates. Producers are at the base of all **food chains**.

Animals are unable to make their own food, so they are **consumers** and depend on the producers, either directly or indirectly, for food. Herbivores are primary consumers that feed on producers. They, in turn, are eaten by carnivores, the meat-eating animals that are hunters. In some food chains there are tertiary consumers. These are predators that prey on other predators, for example the killer whale preys on sea otters, and the mongoose preys on snakes.

THE SCIENCE YOU LEARN: PREDATOR AND PREY

There is a close relationship between the number of prey animals and the predators that hunt them. As can be seen on the graph below, when numbers of prey increase, the predators find more food and their numbers also increase. When the prey numbers fall, the predators starve and their numbers fall. This relationship is important for the conservation of endangered species.

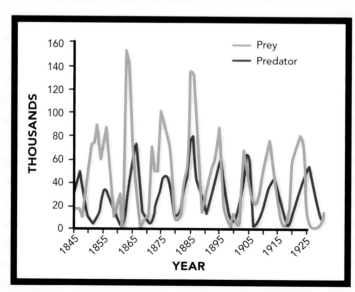

Food chains and food webs

A food chain is a very simple representation of the feeding relationships that exist between plants and animals. For example, grass is eaten by zebras and zebras are eaten by lions.

There are a few examples where animals are totally dependent on one food source, for example the giant panda feeds on bamboo. For these animals, if their food source is wiped out, for example by a forest fire or deforestation, their survival is threatened. However, in most cases animals feed on a range of foods, so their survival is not linked to just one species. For example, lions feed on herbivores such as antelope and wildebeest, and not just zebra. These feeding relationships can be shown as a food web.

CASE STUDY

The sea otter

The sea otter lives along the Pacific Coast of North America. It feeds on abalone, clams, sea urchins, and other marine animals found mostly on the seabed. Since the 1990s, the number of sea otters in Alaska has fallen by 90 percent, and it is now classed as being endangered. Biologists have identified a number of causes, including water pollution and hunting, but surprisingly the main cause is predation by killer whales. The killer whale's more usual diet are sea lions and seals, but their numbers have declined because of overfishing in that area. The killer whales are now taking anything they can find – including sea otters.

Balancing act

The removal of one animal from a food chain or food web affects all the other animals. For example, removal of predators such as lions or leopards from the African **savannah** allows populations of herbivores, such as zebra and wildebeest, to increase. This can lead to overgrazing of the grassland and, over time, the herbivores starve and their numbers decrease.

The conservation of endangered species will only be successful if the species' feeding relationships are considered at the start. There is no point trying to conserve a species if there are insufficient prey animals in the habitat to support it.

Sustainable numbers

The number of individuals in a particular habitat is critical to its management. For example, if there are too few herbivores on grassland, the vegetation may become overgrown. When this happens, the low-growing grasses that herbivores prefer to eat are out-competed by taller, more vigorous plants. On the other hand, if too many animals overgraze the plants, they will run out of food.

In any given habitat, there is an optimum (best possible) number of individuals. This is the **sustainable** number, the number that the habitat can support over a long period of time. It is called the **carrying capacity**.

Too many or too few?

If a particular species is introduced into an area, and the conditions are good, it increases in number. At first, the increase is slow, but as the numbers grow, so does the rate of increase. The increase in population continues so long as there is plenty of food, space, places to shelter, no disease, and few predators. If there is a reduction in one of these factors, for example food supplies dwindle or there are too few roosting sites, the population levels off at the carrying capacity.

The line on this graph shows the number of animals in the habitat. The numbers increase up to the carrying capacity and then they level off.

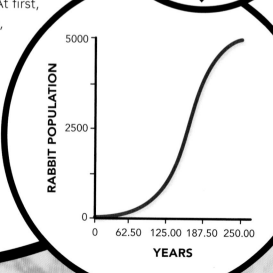

Under pressure

In many countries, the demand for land for agriculture, industry, and urban development is high. This means that animals tend to be confined to protected areas, such as nature reserves and National Parks. If the animals increase in number, they may run out of space and have nowhere else to move.

Hard decisions

In Southern Africa, successful conservation programmes have resulted in elephant numbers increasing. However, the elephants have overgrazed the land. They have pulled down acacia trees to get at leaves and destroyed large areas of scrubland. This has threatened the survival of both the elephant and other species. Difficult decisions have had to be made regarding the future of the elephants. In some places, they have been captured and moved to new areas, but in others, whole herds have been culled (killed) to reduce elephant populations.

CASE STUDY

Too many tigers

The Bengal tiger is endangered and in recent years its population has fallen to less than 2,000. Bandhavgarh National Park in India is a well known tiger reserve, where the numbers of tigers have increased. The park is surrounded by a fence to prevent the tigers and other animals moving onto the surrounding farmland and into villages. Tigers are at the top of the food chain and they need a large territory in which they can hunt. However, there is a lack of space and the park cannot support all the tigers. Young tigers are desperate to leave the park and find their own territory, but there is nowhere for them to go.

This tigress is patrolling the fence around Bandhavgarh National Park. She is three years old, but because she is sharing territory with her mother, she is unable to have her own cubs.

Estimating population size

A population is the number of individuals of a particular species within a specified area, for example the number of snails in a garden. Population sizes are based on estimates, since it is usually impossible to count every single animal or plant within a given area. For example, imagine you have to estimate the number of birds in a large flock. Counting them all would be impossible, so the best approach is to count what appears to be about one-tenth of the flock and then multiply this figure by ten. Other methods involve trapping and marking animals.

INVESTIGATION: CAPTURE AND RECAPTURE

A common and simple method of estimating the numbers of small animals in a given area is the capture and recapture method. It is used by students and researchers around the world to estimate population size.

To estimate the number of woodlice living in a pile of logs, spend about 10 minutes catching woodlice. Mark each one with a white spot so it can be identified again and then release it back onto the log pile. Two days later, repeat the exercise and make a note of the total number caught in 10 minutes, including the number of marked woodlice. Use the formula below to estimate the population size.

Population size = (number marked in first sample) x (total caught in second sample) ÷ (number marked in second sample)

For example, 100 woodlice were caught, marked, and released. Two days later 150 woodlice were caught, including 50 marked woodlice. So:

Population size = (100 x 150) ÷ 50 = 240

Snails' shells can be marked with tiny spots of white paint so they can be identified when recaptured.

Studying blue crabs in Chesapeake Bay

A capture-recapture method was chosen by biologists studying blue crabs in Chesapeake Bay in the United States. The number of blue crabs in the bay had fallen due to over-fishing. Biologists want to boost the population by raising young crabs in a hatchery and releasing them into the wild.

First, the biologists had to estimate the number of wild crabs that were already living in the area, using the capture-recapture method. They caught a number of adult blue crabs, marked them with a tag and then released them. The crabs were recaptured over the next few months by local fishermen, in exchange for a reward. This gave the biologists the figures they needed to work out the numbers of adult crabs and decide how many young crabs they needed to release into the bay to boost the population.

Tagging was used at the next stage of the project, too. The biologists wanted to know if the hatchery-raised crabs would survive in the wild. They were concerned that hatchery crabs would not know which foods to eat and how to hide from predators, such as fish. Before they were released, the young crabs were double tagged with a plastic tag that could be seen through the semi-transparent crab shells and an internal electronic tag that carried information, such as dates and weight, etc. During the months following their release, the biologists trawled areas of the seabed to catch the young crabs and record their growth.

This brown bear has been tagged in both ears. This enables researchers to identify the animal from a distance.

Managing habitats

Conservation is not just about protecting, it is all about management. It is relatively easy to buy a piece of grassland or woodland in order to protect the species that live within it. However, unless the area is managed correctly, changes may occur that threaten the very survival of the protected species.

For example, chalk grassland is home to many species of rare butterflies that depend on low-growing plants. If left alone, the grassland soon becomes scrub (see panel on **succession**) and the butterflies lose their habitat. To prevent this happening, the grassland has to be managed. Sheep can be used to graze the grass and prevent trees and shrubs from growing.

In southern England, **heathland** is home to the endangered sand lizard. Heathland is soon overrun by pine trees, so to protect the sand lizards' habitat, pine tree seedlings have to be removed. This can be done by hand, but an easier way is to burn the heathland in a carefully controlled fashion. The heathers regrow, but the pine seedlings are killed.

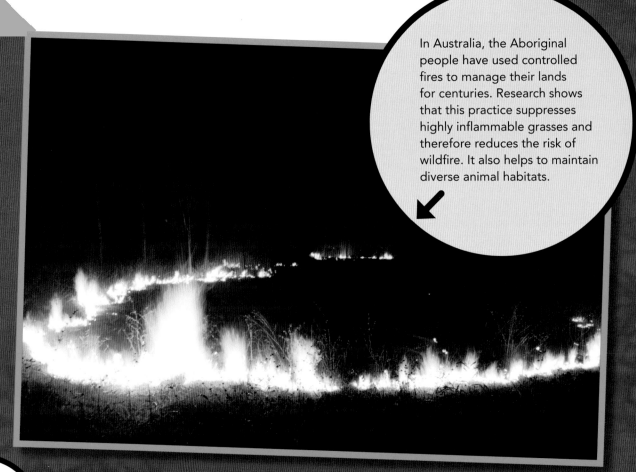

In Australia, the Aboriginal people have used controlled fires to manage their lands for centuries. Research shows that this practice suppresses highly inflammable grasses and therefore reduces the risk of wildfire. It also helps to maintain diverse animal habitats.

Woodland management

Woodlands have to be managed, too. Woodland trees cast a lot of shade and this stops plants from becoming established on the woodland floor. When a large tree blows over, a gap is created. This allows smaller plants to start to grow which increases the biodiversity of the woodland. Gaps can be created artificially by felling (chopping down) small areas of trees to create glades (open spaces) and rides (paths). Different plants live in these sunny areas and they attract different animals into the woodland. This means that woodland with glades and rides has more wildlife living in it than woodland with no open spaces.

THE SCIENCE YOU LEARN: SUCCESSION

Succession is the term used to describe the changes in habitat that occur when an area of bare ground becomes colonised with plants.
❶ The first plants to become established on bare ground are low-growing plants such as grasses. ❷ Then the taller plants arrive, such as shrubs, and they shade out the grasses. ❸ The grassland gradually becomes scrub land. ❹ More time passes and tree species become established.
❺ The trees grow taller than the shrubs, and woodland develops.
❻ The woodland is the final part of the succession, called the climax vegetation. ❼ Woodlands are stable habitats that survive for hundreds of years, unless damaged by fire or storm, or cleared by people. If this happens, then the succession starts all over again

Forest Succession

1   2   3   4   5   6   7

Recreating habitats

Natural habitats are being cleared all the time, especially forests, and they are replaced by farmland, houses, and industry. Often, it is necessary to recreate habitats in order to conserve plants and animals.

New wetlands

Wetland habitats, such as marshes, fens, mangrove swamps, and ponds, are frequently drained to make way for development or farmland. Wetlands are important habitats as they have a high biodiversity, supporting both terrestrial (land) and aquatic (water) species. Amphibians, for example, have suffered particularly as a result of the loss of freshwater habitats and the increase in water pollution. Fortunately, wetlands can be recreated. New ponds can be dug in the corners of fields, in parks and in gardens. Sometimes, it is possible to flood low-lying land to recreate marshes and water meadows. Not only does this benefit wildlife, it also helps to prevent flooding.

Mangrove swamps are found along many tropical coasts and they are important habitats for fish and birds. They act as fish nurseries and as natural storm barriers, protecting the inland areas from tidal surges (periodic rises in sea level). Many mangroves were cleared to make way for new ports and holiday developments, but now they are being replanted as people realise just how important they are.

This newly-planted mangrove swamp will provide vital protection to a stretch of coastline in Indonesia.

These volunteers are planting trees in an area that was deforested in Costa Rica, South America.

Replanting forests

Today, about six percent of the world's land surface is covered by tropical rainforests, and they are home to half the world's species. Although this may seem a large area, it is less than half the total area of rainforest that once existed, and more rainforest is being cleared every year.

Rainforest forms over hundreds of years, so once it is cleared it takes many years to recreate this wonderful habitat. However, rainforests can be replanted for the future. The replanted forests, known as secondary forests, are not as dark as the original forests. This enables species that prefer more light, such as vines and other climbing plants, to become established. In turn, these plants attract a different range of insects and birds. In time the trees grow taller and cast more shade, and the forest becomes more like the original primary forest.

IN YOUR HOME: CREATE A MEADOW

A lawn is formed from grasses and other low-growing plants that can survive being cut each week. Grass leaves grow from the base so are not harmed by cutting, while low-growing rosette plants, such as the daisy, are missed by the blades of the lawn mower. If a lawn is left uncut, the grasses grow tall and shade out the rosette plants, which die out and are replaced by more grasses.

Meadows are grassy habitats where the grasses and other plants can grow tall. Each year, the grasses are cut for hay. This happens in mid to late summer, once the plants have flowered and dispersed their seeds. A meadow can be recreated in the garden by simply allowing an area of grass to grow long and only cutting it once or twice a year. For more interest, native meadow flowers, such as ox-eye daisy, can be planted among the grass.

Coping with climate change

Biologists managing habitats for wildlife are facing new challenges. In the past they had to deal with the problems of habitat loss, acid rain damaging trees, and pests and diseases threatening rare species. Today, they have to cope with the changes linked to increasing climate change.

Extreme weather

Some species are vulnerable because they only exist in one small area, and if anything happens to their habitat, the species could be wiped out. For example, the Jamaican giant swallowtail butterfly lives in just a few areas of rainforest on the island of Jamaica. Hurricanes occur in the Caribbean every year, and they damage buildings and trees. One of the consequences of global warming is weather becoming more extreme. It is predicted that hurricanes will become stronger and more common. If a devastating hurricane destroys the forests in which the giant swallowtail lives, the species could be threatened.

Weather patterns are changing, too. Areas of the world such as Australia and parts of the United States are experiencing long droughts. In Australia, bush fires have spread through woodlands, threatening endangered **marsupials**, such as koalas, that depend on eucalyptus trees.

A firefighting plane dumps its cargo of red liquid in an attempt to bring a forest fire under control.

Some animals and plants live in close partnership with each other, with both partners benefiting from the relationship. This is called mutualism. One example of mutualism is hard corals and algae. Hard corals are responsible for building coral reefs. The algae live in the cells of the corals, providing them with food, while the corals give the algae shelter. The algae also give the coral animals their colour.

However, global warming is causing a slight increase in sea temperature, and this is causing the algae to leave the corals. When this happens, the corals lose their food source and slowly starve to death. They also lose their colour and turn white, a process known as coral bleaching. This has devastating effects on the many fish and other aquatic species that live among the coral.

Coral bleaching has been seen on most coral reefs around the world. The coral and marine populations can recover, but many do not. It is thought that a quarter of the world's coral reefs have already been lost to coral bleaching

This fan coral has been bleached after a slight rise in the temperature of the sea.

Rising temperatures

Global warming has resulted in many ice caps and glaciers melting more rapidly, and flooding is predicted to become more common as the world's sea levels rise. Low-lying areas around the Bay of Bengal in the northern Indian Ocean are susceptible to flooding, both from fresh water carried down by the Ganges and Brahmaputra Rivers, and from salt water blown in by tropical cyclones. When flooding occurs, it is not just the people that suffer – the wildlife living in the flood areas suffers, too.

Conservation versus hunting

People have always hunted animals. However, excessive hunting has made numerous species extinct and pushed many others to the brink of extinction. Despite public outcry, the hunting of animals for products such as fur, ivory, and bone, still continues.

Fur trade

Animals such as mink, leopard, beaver, seal, and otter are all killed for their fur, which is made into coats and other items of clothing. There are international laws to control the trade in endangered animals, and many countries have laws banning the hunting of threatened species. However, the trade continues illegally.

Hunting versus tourism

Tanzania is a poor African country with a large population, but more than 40 per cent of the land area is protected. Wildlife conservation is a big issue for the Tanzanian government as it represents a valuable asset that provides many jobs and earns the country a lot of money. However, much of this money comes from big game hunters who want to shoot large animals and take home a trophy, rather than from tourists watching animals.

Big game hunting is thriving in Tanzania. Much of the protected land lies in inaccessible areas that are plagued by tsetse flies that carry the disease sleeping sickness. These are lands that are not suitable for the average tourist. However, big game hunters are happy to travel to these areas. They pay as much as US$50,000 to shoot one rhino or elephant. This raises a conservation dilemma. Which is better – big game hunters or tourists? A lot of tourists would be needed to raise that amount of money and they could do more damage to the environment than one hunter and a support team. But is it right to encourage people who want to shoot animals for fun?

One animal under threat is the Tibetan antelope, which is hunted for its very fine wool. Unfortunately, the antelope cannot be sheared like domestic sheep, as the hairs have to be pulled out, so it is shot and its skin removed. The wool is made into a shawl called a shahtoosh that is sold illegally to rich people living in Hong Kong, London, New York, and other cities.

Big game hunting

A century ago, big game hunting was a popular activity. Wealthy Europeans and Americans went to Africa to shoot animals, such as lion and elephant. However, they shot so many that these "trophy" animals almost disappeared. National Parks were set up and big game hunting stopped. Today, conservationists are facing a dilemma – should controlled hunting be allowed in order to conserve wildlife? In some places, there are too many elephants and they need to be killed (see page 13). Is it better to allow the wealthy hunters to pay large sums of money to kill the animals and use the money for conservation?

This elephant with its long tusks is an impressive sight. Allowing hunters to shoot a few elephants could help to conserve many other animals.

Captive breeding

One way to ensure the survival of a threatened species is to collect individuals from the wild and keep them in captivity. Sometimes, this is done alongside conservation programmes such as habitat protection, but for a few species it has been a last attempt to ensure their survival.

Captive breeding programmes keep the animals in zoos and wildlife parks where they breed and increase in number. Eventually, some animals can be released back into their natural habitat. However, for some species, the chances of being released into the wild are very slim as their habitat has disappeared.

Looking after the animals

The days when zoos put animals in small concrete pens are now long gone. Today, the animals are given lots of space and the keepers try to recreate conditions that are similar to their natural habitat. Animals such as the gorillas are kept in family groups and they are given lots of toys and activities to keep them occupied. Some species breed well in captivity, for example the Siberian tiger, and now there are more living in captivity than in the wild. However, other species are very difficult to breed in captivity, for example the giant panda.

Costly exercise

Keeping large animals in captivity is expensive and they produce only small numbers of offspring, so captive breeding programmes take many years. By contrast, keeping invertebrates, such as insects, is much easier. The London Zoo has a captive breeding programme for the Wartbiter cricket, a vulnerable insect with just a few wild populations left in Britain. Crickets reared by the zoo are released to boost the wild populations.

Wartbiter crickets like tussocky grassland where there are few grazing animals. Habitat loss has led to the species' decline across Northern Europe, especially in the United Kingdom.

Careful breeding

Biologists have to be careful that the animals do not mate with related individuals (**inbreed**), as this would weaken the species. The aim is to maintain the most genetically diverse population possible. This is achieved by studying the genetic backgrounds of the captive animals and choosing the best partners. Often, the zoos maintain a "stud book" with details of the parentage of the captive animals. This means that each breeding centre can pick the best male for their breeding females and arrange exchanges of individual animals.

California condor

The California condor (right) is a scavenging bird that feeds on carrion (the dead remains of animals). During the 1970s, the population of condors fell to just 22. One of the main causes of this decline in numbers was lead poisoning. The condors were taking in lead shot when they fed on dead animals that had been shot by hunters. Biologists decided that the only way to save the species was to capture all of them and keep them in captivity. The breeding programme was organized by the San Diego Wild Animal Park, Los Angeles Zoo, and The Peregrine Fund. Fortunately, the

condors adjusted well to captivity and started to breed. By 1996, there were enough condors to release some back into the wild at four locations in California, Baja California, and Arizona. The release of captive birds will continue for some time, until the condor population in the wild is sustainable.

Seed banks

Plants are much easier to conserve for the future. This is because seeds can be collected and then stored in carefully controlled conditions. Seeds are produced by sexual reproduction in plants. A seed consists of a tough seed coat that encloses an **embryo** and a store of food. The seed remains in a dormant (inactive) state until it experiences the right conditions for **germination**, and then it starts to grow. Some seeds can only be kept for a few weeks before they lose the ability to germinate, but others can remain **viable** (able to germinate) for hundreds of years.

THE SCIENCE YOU LEARN: SEED GERMINATION

It is important that seeds only germinate when the conditions are right for their growth. To prevent them germinating at the wrong time or in the wrong place, seeds have to be kept in controlled conditions. All seeds need water and oxygen to germinate. Some need warm temperatures, while others may require a long period of cold temperatures. Seeds with hard seed coats may have to pass through the gut of an animal first. This breaks down the seed coat so that water can be taken up by the seed. A few seeds will only germinate after a forest fire, when the smoke from the fire triggers the germination process.

When a seed germinates, it takes up water so that the seed coat splits. Then a root and shoot appear.

Seeds for the future

The largest seed bank in the world for wild species is the Millennium Seed Bank of The Royal Botanic Gardens at Kew in London. This seed bank works with partners all over the world, such as the Botanical Gardens in Budapest, Hungary, the Seeds of Success Program in the United States, and the Royal Botanic Gardens, Sydney, Australia. The partners collect seeds which are sent to the Millennium Seed Bank, where they are identified, cleaned, and dried. The seeds are then packaged and placed in storage at a temperature of just below freezing. Every few years, the seeds are checked and a few germinated, to check they are still viable. Sometimes, a few seeds are germinated and grown into plants, so that fresh seed can be collected. This project has already stored seed from 10 percent of the world's known seed-producing plants, some of which are extinct in the wild.

In a seed storage warehouse, glass containers have been filled with cleaned seeds. They are stored at low temperatures until required.

Reintroducing lost animals

The ultimate aim of a captive breeding programme is to release animals back into the wild. However, this is only possible if the right conditions can be established for the animals' survival. In recent years, a number of endangered species have been reintroduced to their former habitat, including the white-tailed eagle in Europe and Przewalski's horse in Mongolia.

At the start of the nineteenth century, there were as many as 100 million American bison roaming the prairies of North America. By the 1880s, hunting had reduced the numbers to just a few hundred. The species was saved from extinction by a few ranchers who rescued some of the buffalo and bred them on their ranches. Today, there are about 500,000 bison, some in National Parks such as Yellowstone in the United States, but the majority are captive animals kept for their meat and skin.

CUTTING EDGE: WILD HORSES

Przewalski's horse (see photo below) is the world's only wild horse and it roamed the grasslands of Mongolia. During the 1960s, it became extinct in the wild. Fortunately, a small herd was kept in captivity and, after thirty years and thirteen generations of horses, some Przewalski's horses were released back into a protected habitat in Mongolia. In 2005 there were an estimated 300 horses in the wild.

Reintroducing birds

Unlike many mammals, birds tend to adapt more easily to captivity and their breeding rate tends to be quicker. There are examples of several successful bird re-introductions, including the Hawaiian goose, or Ne-Ne, and the brown teal in New Zealand. In Europe, the white-tailed eagle has made a comeback. Numbers of this majestic bird fell to just a few pairs during the 1960s, but today there are hundreds. Conservation has involved protecting the breeding birds from egg collectors, and the purchase of forests and lakes where the birds breed and hunt. These efforts have also benefited other species that live in the forests.

CASE STUDY

Reintroducing the wolf

The wolf has always had a bad press. It has been portrayed as an evil animal that kills people and livestock (farm animals such as cattle, sheep, pigs, and goats). As a result, wolf populations were hunted and only a few now remain in Europe and North America. In reality, the wolf is not that much of a threat to people, and in places such as India and Eastern Europe, wolves live close to people. Now there are plans to reintroduce the wolf into parts of its former range in Scotland and the United States. A reintroduction has several advantages – the wolves help to control the numbers of animals, such as deer, which have increased due to a lack of natural predators, and they attract tourists. However, local people need to be persuaded that wolves are good for the environment. Many people fear the wolves will attack their animals, both livestock and pets. In Norway, wolves have become re-established naturally, and farmers are reporting that sheep are being attacked.

Studying animal behaviour

As well as studying an animal's requirements in terms of habitat and food, it is important to understand an animal's behaviour, especially when planning a re-introduction.

Some animals live on their own (for example the giant panda) and only come into contact with other members of the same species to breed. By watching giant pandas, biologists discovered how the males reacted to each other and why many males failed to find a mate. This information has helped to improve the breeding success of captive pandas.

Many animals live in social groups, so a reintroduction programme needs to take this into account. For example, wolves and African hunting dogs live in packs. Each pack has a dominant, or top, male and female. The dominant pair leads the rest of the pack on hunts, and is first to eat.

Balanced populations

When a reintroduced population is being established, it is important to get the correct balance of ages and sexes. For example, when reintroducing birds such as the white-tailed eagle, it is best to introduce a small number of birds over a number of years, rather than a single reintroduction of young birds. This will establish a population with a mix of sexes and ages.

African hunting dogs live in packs that hunt together. Once a pack finds prey, the dogs work as a team to make the kill.

Observing chimpanzees

Anthropologist, Dr Jane Goodall (pictured left, in 1972) is a leading expert in the behaviour of chimpanzees. As a young researcher, she studied chimps in the Gombe Game Reserve, Tanzania. At the time, little was known about chimps. Every day Jane followed a troop of chimps into the forest, recording everything about their behaviour. Gradually, the chimps became used to her and allowed her to get close to them. Jane was able to learn much about the animals, such as their relationships with each other and their daily routines.

Removing individuals

Knowledge of animal behaviour is important if it becomes necessary to remove animals from a population, for example if there are too many in an area. Depending on the species, it may be necessary to remove or even kill all the members of a family group, rather than just remove a few members. For example, elephants live in tight-knit family groups and it is kinder to move or kill the entire family. In other species, killing one or two of the dominant members may result in the others suffering because they cannot find food or they fight among themselves.

 ## IN YOUR HOME: ADAPTING TO HUMAN HABITATS

Many animals are quick to learn new patterns of behaviour, and can adapt well to new habitats and feeding opportunities. Pigeons, gulls, rats, and mice have all learned to live alongside people, taking advantage of food found in bins and on rubbish tips. In North America, brown bears have learned that camp sites and car parks are good places to find food. Signs warn tourists to lock their car doors and windows, use bear-proof bins, and keep any food in secure bear-proof containers.

Genetics and conservation

Ecology is not the only subject that is important for protecting endangered species. In recent years, an understanding of genetics is proving to be essential for conservation and for planning breeding programmes.

Inheritance

Genetics is the study of inheritance. It looks at how characteristics are passed from one generation to the next through the **genes**, which are units of genetic information. A gene is made up of a length of a chemical called deoxyribonucleic acid, or **DNA**. DNA forms the **chromosomes**. Each chromosome is a single, tightly coiled DNA molecule.

Each species has a specific number of chromosomes in their cells, and each chromosome carries many genes. For example, humans have 23 pairs of chromosomes and between 20,000–25,000 genes.

Most animals and plants reproduce sexually. This means that two sets of genes, one from the father and one from the mother, fuse to create a new animal or plant. In humans, sperm contain 23 chromosomes and an egg contains 23 chromosomes. When a sperm fertilizes the egg, the resultant embryo has 23 chromosomes from each parent – the full set of 23 pairs – and a combination of their characteristics.

Chromosomes

Nucleus

In a human cell, the chromosomes are packed into the nucleus.

Cell

Code breaking

Each length of DNA that makes up a gene carries a code. This code contains all the information needed by the cell to make proteins. Proteins are essential building blocks in the body and they have many roles, including structural components, transport proteins such as haemoglobin (which carries oxygen in the blood), and **enzymes** that control chemical reactions. In 2003, the Human Genome Project successfully mapped all the genes in the human body and worked out the sequence of all the chemicals that make up the codes. Now scientists are studying the DNA of other species.

THE SCIENCE YOU LEARN: DOMINANT AND RECESSIVE ALLELES

Genes exist in two forms, or **alleles**, and these are usually dominant and recessive. The presence of these alleles controls the outward appearance of the individual, with the **dominant allele** masking the **recessive allele**. An individual may have two dominant alleles, two recessive alleles, or one of each. For example, Bengal tigers are orange with black stripes, but very occasionally a white tiger is born. The orange allele is dominant and the white allele is recessive. An orange tiger usually has two dominant alleles and a white tiger has two recessive alleles. However, there are a few carriers – tigers that have one dominant allele and one recessive allele, which is masked or hidden. If two carrier tigers mate, there is a one-in-four chance they will produce a white tiger.

In this diagram, the allele for an orange coat is represented by T, and the allele for a white coat is represented by t. Both parents have one orange and one white allele (Tt). Half their gametes carry the orange allele and half carry the white allele. If two Tt tigers breed together, then four different pairings can result: TT, Tt, Tt, and tt. This means that three-quarters of their cubs are likely to have orange coats, and one-quarter to have white coats.

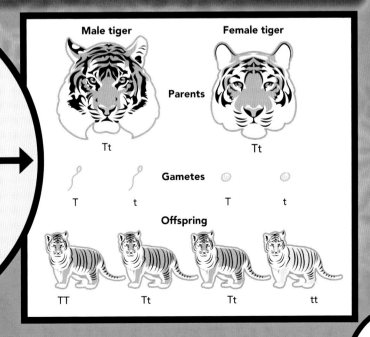

Genetic diversity

Look at any group of people, and you will see that they are all slightly different. They differ in many ways, including height, hair, skin, and eye colour. Despite these differences, all people belong to the human species *Homo sapiens*. These differences between individuals of the same species are known as **variation**.

Variation

Variation in a species is important, as the tiny differences contribute to a species' ability to survive in times of change. If you look at a field of wheat, you see that the plants all look the same, with similar numbers and sizes of seeds. This is because the plants are genetically similar. The genetic uniformity helps to increase yield (the number of crops grown), but it also makes the crop vulnerable as one disease could wipe out the whole crop. If the plants were more variable, there would be a greater chance of some plants being resistant to the disease and surviving.

The same principle applies to animal populations. If there is a small population of breeding animals, there is a greater chance of inbreeding. This is when animals breed with close relatives. Inbreeding produces offspring that are genetically similar, so they are not as healthy as individuals that have been bred by genetically different parents. The offspring may not grow as large or live as long, and may even suffer from genetic diseases.

Inbreeding in tigers

There are fewer than 200 white tigers in the world, and they all live in zoos. During the 1950s, a male white tiger called Mohan was captured in India. He was kept in captivity and bred with orange female tigers in the hope of producing more white tigers. White tigers were rare and very valuable, so people were keen to breed them. However, the attempts were unsuccessful until they bred Mohan with a closely related female, who was a carrier of the white coat allele. She produced four white cubs that were used in breeding programmes around the world.

The offspring of these four white tiger cubs have become very inbred, as they have been mated to close family members. Today, the tigers born as a result of this inbreeding suffer from many health problems, for example cubs are often stillborn or die soon after birth, while other cubs have deformed skeletons and kidney problems. Zoos are trying to improve the genetic **diversity** of their white tigers by mating them with orange tigers to produce carriers (tigers that are orange but which carry the recessive white allele) and then mating these carrier tigers with unrelated white tigers.

DNA fingerprinting

In recent years, scientists have perfected a technique that enables them to identify an individual from his or her DNA, and to work out whether different individuals are related to each other.

THE SCIENCE YOU LEARN: DNA FINGERPRINTING

A DNA fingerprint is obtained by chopping up a sample of DNA into small fragments using enzymes called restriction enzymes. The fragments are of different lengths and they are sorted by size using a process called gel electrophoresis. The fragments cannot be seen, so radioactive markers are added to the fragments. When a piece of photographic paper is placed over the fragments, the markers show up as black lines. The result is a DNA fingerprint that is made up of a series of bars of differing thickness, that looks a bit like a bar code.

A person's fingerprint is unique, so it can be used for identification purposes. Now scientists have developed a technique that enables them to take a sample of DNA from an individual and create a **genetic fingerprint**. Genetic fingerprints have proved to be invaluable for forensic scientists (scientists who carry out investigations in order to give evidence in a court of law). They take samples of DNA from hair, skin, and other body tissues found at a crime scene, and use them to identify the criminal.

DNA fingerprinting in the field

Fortunately, these advances in biology in the laboratory can be used by biologists working in the field. For example, DNA fingerprinting has been used in India to estimate tiger populations. It is difficult to count tigers in thick jungle, and the same individual may be counted twice, pushing the population estimates too high. Tigers can also be identified from the pattern of their stripes, but you have to be able to see the tiger first. Now biologists can identify a tiger by extracting DNA from its dung. Although it is an expensive method, knowing which tiger produced the dung enables biologists to estimate population, size of territory, and how family members are dispersed (spread out) through an area. Genetic fingerprinting has also been used by zoos and other breeding centres to identify suitable parents in their breeding programme, to avoid the problems of inbreeding.

Fingerprinting and classification

Biologists are discovering new species all the time, especially in rainforests where only a fraction of the species has been discovered. Traditionally, an unknown organism, such as a plant, would be **classified** using its external characteristics, such as shape of leaves, the colour and number of petals, and the number of stamens. It would then be placed in the same family as other plants of a similar appearance. Genetic fingerprinting is proving to be critical in this process. DNA analyses are showing that plants that look very similar are not necessarily related and, conversely, that plants with very different flowers can be closely related. These studies are rewriting the way biologists classify species.

Changing populations

Environments have always changed. There have been periods in the Earth's history which were much colder, and other periods when the climate was warmer. However, the shifts in climate that are happening today are occurring more quickly than in the past. Many species are having difficulty in adapting to these changes in such a short time.

The comma butterfly is benefiting from global warming because winters are getting warmer so it can survive in more northerly areas.

Adapting to changes

Global warming is already changing environments. There are more droughts, floods, and warmer winters. Some plants are flowering earlier in the year, before their **pollinators** (for instance, insects or birds) have hatched, leaving insects such as butterflies without their food plant. But some species are benefiting from the changes. These are the adaptable species that can change their habitat or food supply. They are likely to have greater genetic diversity, so that some individuals are able to survive and reproduce. They pass their genes onto the next generation, who inherit this feature. Species that are less adaptable are likely to die out, for example they may be unable to move to find food, or are too closely linked to a specific pollinator or food plant. When the changes affect their habitat, they are unable to adapt and eventually they become extinct.

Smilodon, a sabre-toothed cat, was adept at bringing down young, old, or sick mammoths. But when the mammoths became extinct (around 12,800 years ago), so did the *Smilodon*. This is a classic case of co-extinction.

Generalist or specialist?

The life cycle of the butterfly involves **metamorphosis**. The egg hatches into a larva – a worm-like animal without wings. The larva then pupates, forming a cocoon around itself. Within the cocoon, the larva changes into the adult butterfly.

Butterflies have to adapt to environmental changes just like other animals. Some species of butterfly are specialists because they lay their eggs on specific food plants, so they only live in habitats where this plant occurs. If their food plant dies out, so does the butterfly. Generalist butterflies lay their eggs on very common plants or on a range of plants. This enables them to live in a variety of habitats. For example, the small tortoiseshell (*Aglais urticae*) lays its eggs on nettles, while the cabbage white (*Pieris brassicae*) lays its eggs on cabbage plants.

THE SCIENCE YOU LEARN: SPECIATION

Sometimes, a small group of individuals of the same species become separated from the rest of the population, for example they may be separated by a river or a large motorway, or they may be blown across the sea. When this happens, they have to breed among themselves. They may develop differences in appearance or change their behaviour. In time, the new population becomes so different that it can no longer breed with the rest of the species – they have become a new species. This process, whereby a new species is formed, is called **speciation.**

Reproductive biology

The main objective of keeping an endangered species in a captive breeding programme is to create the conditions in which it will breed successfully. As well as understanding the species' needs in terms of their food, social grouping, and environment, biologists need to understand the species' reproductive cycle.

Fertility

Female mammals are not fertile (able to produce offspring) all the time. For example, female gorillas are fertile for a few days every month, while lions are fertile for five days in every sixteen days, and wolves are fertile for just two weeks in every year. Knowledge of when a female mammal will be fertile, and of the signs that she is fertile, is essential, so that male mammals can be mated with her at the right time.

The length of time an animal is pregnant is called the **gestation period**. This also varies from mammal to mammal. Marsupials known as opossums have a short gestation period of just 11 to 13 days. Their young are born very undeveloped and complete their development in their mother's pouch. In contrast, the African elephant is pregnant for up to 660 days (nearly two years) and gives birth to a single, well developed calf that can stand up and feed within minutes of being born. In a breeding programme, a mammal with a short gestation period and large litters (offspring produced from a single birth) enables large numbers of animals to be produced in a relatively short period of time. However, endangered species such as elephants and rhino reproduce very slowly. This is one of the reasons why they are endangered, as hunting has killed more animals than could be replaced by breeding.

 THE SCIENCE YOU LEARN: REPRODUCTIVE HORMONES

Reproduction in mammals is controlled by **hormones**. Hormones are chemical messengers that are released from glands in the body. They travel in the blood to target organs, where they bring about an effect.

For example, in humans, four hormones control the 28-day reproductive cycle in women – oestrogen and progesterone from the ovary, and follicle-stimulating hormone and luteinising hormone from the brain.

Zhanga the giant panda gave birth to her cub in the Wolong Nature Reserve, China, in 2006.

Helping giant pandas

Giant pandas have proved to be very difficult to breed in captivity. Often, they showed no interest in mating or they were very aggressive to each other. Studies found that female giant pandas are only fertile for a few days once a year. Now biologists can predict when a female panda is fertile from the levels of the hormones oestrogen and progesterone in her urine. Once oestrogen starts to increase, peak fertility occurs in about 10 days. After mating has taken place, there is further monitoring of hormones in the urine to see if the female panda is pregnant, using a pregnancy testing kit similar to that used by human females. The gestation period ranges from 84 to 160 days in captivity. Since it is so variable, keepers have learned to recognise the signs that a female is about to give birth. Now the breeding success rate has improved so much that there are enough giant pandas to release back into the wild.

Giving a helping hand

Knowledge of human reproduction has improved greatly in recent years, with doctors being able to give fertility treatment to infertile couples and carry out embryo **implantation** (see panel). This knowledge is also being used by veterinarians to treat animals in captivity.

Artificial insemination

Artificial insemination (AI) involves collecting sperm from male animals and injecting it into the uterus of the female animal when she is fertile. AI has long been carried out on livestock such as cattle and pigs, as it avoids the need to transport the male to the female. It also means that the sperm of a particularly fine male can be used on many more females around the world than would be possible naturally.

CUTTING EDGE: EMBRYO IMPLANTATION

Embryonic implantation involves biologists taking an egg from a female and fertilizing it in the laboratory. The resulting embryo is placed into the uterus of the same or another female animal, where it develops normally. This procedure is carried out on infertile women and on valuable livestock such as cattle.

Embryonic implantation could be used for endangered animals, too, but first research is needed to make sure the procedure will work. However, it is not easy to carry out the research on endangered species as there are too few animals, so related animals are used instead. The Striped-Faced Dunnart (right) is a common marsupial from Australia with a gestation period of just 11 to 12 days, the shortest of any mammal. It also releases up to 30 eggs at a time. These characteristics make it perfect for research. The various procedures such as embryo implantation can be practised on the Dunnart's eggs before being attempted on more endangered species.